Let's Play
Tag!

📖 Read the Page

▶ Read the Story

🔄 Repeat

⬛ Stop

⭐ Game

⭐ Level 1 ⭐⭐ Level 2 ⭐⭐⭐ Level 3

💻

TO USE THIS BOOK WITH THE TAG™ READER you must download audio from the LeapFrog Connect application.
The LeapFrog Connect application can be installed from the CD provided with your Tag Reader or at leapfrog.com/tag.

T. Rex's Mighty ROAR

written by Ron Lytle and Scott Sonneborn

illustrated by David Krentz

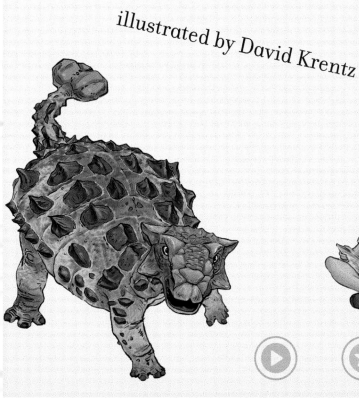

It was a great day for roaring.
So that's just what T. Rex and his
mother did.

ROAR!

ROAR!

After roaring all morning, T. Rex's mother went to find some food.

T. Rex was supposed to wait quietly until she came back.

But he wanted to roar some more.

A dragonfly flew past. T. Rex chased it onto a log and gave it a big

ROAR!

T. Rex roared so loudly, it shook the log.
It broke and fell into the river. Splash!

T. Rex didn't have time to wonder
where he was going.

A flock of flying pterosaurs zoomed towards him. He ducked, and they whooshed right over his head.

When he looked up, he was back on land.

And a pack of Troodon was staring at him with their big, scary eyes.

T. Rex ran into the dark forest. He didn't know where he was. And where was his mother? He roared as loud as he could. Maybe she would hear him.

Sure enough, something roared back. But it wasn't his mother. It was a big, mean Ankylosaurus!

T. Rex ran so fast he tripped over his own legs. He tumbled down a hill and rolled past a Triceratops.

He landed in a nest full of eggs. They belonged to a very big and very angry Alamosaurus!

There was no place for T. Rex to hide.

There was only one thing he could do.

He opened his mouth and ROARED!

And the Alamosaurus ran away.

Then T. Rex saw that something was behind him.

His mother. Her roar scared the Alamosaurus away.

T. Rex was very glad they were together
again. It really had been a great day
for roaring.

Micropachycephalosaurus

Therizinosaurus

small

big

big
fast
long
small
cool

Dinosaur Hall of Fame

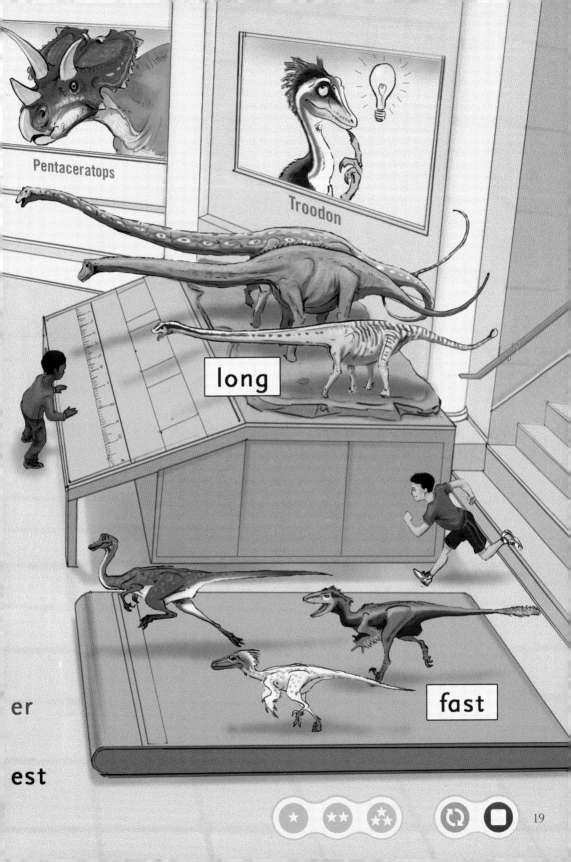

Pentaceratops

Troodon

long

fast

er

est

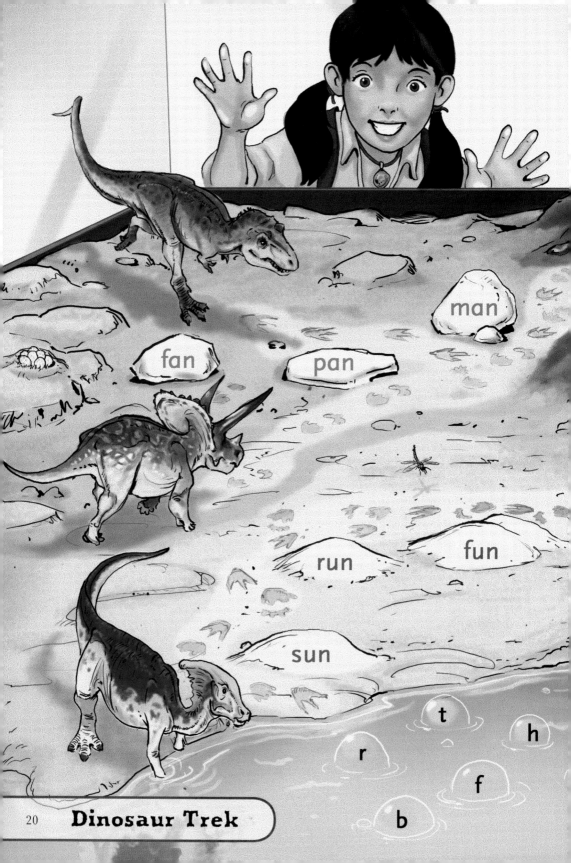

Dinosaur Trek

Hungry Giants

23

CRETACEOUS
146-65 million years ago

Quetzalcoatlus

Parasaurolophus

Troodon

Ankylosaurus

JURASSIC
200-146 million years ago

Archaeopteryx

Stegosaurus

Allosaurus

Compsognathus

TRIASSIC
251-200 million years ago

Eoraptor

Coelophysis

Plateosaurus

The Amazing Mesozoic

Tyrannosaurus Rex

Triceratops

Alamosaurus

Brachiosaurus

egg   neck
plate horn
legs   wings
dragonfly
herbivore
carnivore

25